C A T

T R E A T S

C A T

T R E A T S

Kim Campbell Thornton
&
Jane Calloway

Illustrations by Mark Matcho

Main Street Books
Doubleday

New York
London
Toronto
Sydney
Auckland

A MAIN STREET BOOK
PUBLISHED BY DOUBLEDAY

a division of Bantam Doubleday Dell Publishing Group, Inc.
1540 Broadway, New York, New York 10036

MAIN STREET BOOKS, DOUBLEDAY, and the portrayal of a building with a tree are trademarks
of Doubleday, a division of Bantam Doubleday Dell Publishing Group, Inc.

Design by Amanda Kavanagh, ARK design
Images of tablecloth & cat © 1996 PhotoDisc, Inc.

Library of Congress Cataloging-in-Publication Data
Thornton, Kim Campbell.
    Cat treats / Kim Campbell Thornton and Jane Calloway.—
    1st Main Street Books ed.
        p.   cm.
    1. Cats—Food—Recipes.   2. Cats—Nutrition.   3. Cats.   I. Calloway, Jane.   II. Title.
SF4476.T48   1997
636.8'0852—dc21   96-52952
                                                                          CIP

ISBN 0-385-48461-5
Copyright © 1997 Kim Campbell Thornton and Jane Calloway
All Rights Reserved
Printed in the United States of America
October 1997
First Edition
10 9 8 7 6 5 4 3 2 1

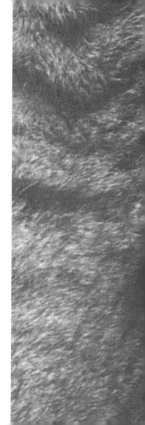

Acknowledgments

Our deepest thanks go to Michael G. Abdella, D.V.M., who reviewed the health and nutrition information in this book and never turned down a dinner invitation; Daryl Teshima; Karen Thomas of Critters of the Cinema; Daniel Q. Estep, Ph.D., and Suzanne Hetts, Ph.D., of Animal Behavior Associates in Littleton, Colorado; and to testers (and tasters) Moira Harris and Rex and Max; Liz Palika and Tigger; Audrey Pavia and Simba and Murray; Ellyce Kaluf and Flea; Doreen Frost and Harley and Black Jack; Kay Clark (thanks, Mom!); Jerry Thornton, our photographer; Debbie Phillips-Donaldson, group editor of *Cat Fancy* magazine; and of course our own Moscow, Shelby, Peter and Pandora, all of whom were willing to try just about anything.

Contents

Introduction

Cat lovers are famous for pampering their feline friends. These furry wonders eat the best food, wear the most fashionable collars, play with the latest rage in cat toys, climb the tallest scratching posts and sleep in the spots of their choosing—all with the blessing of the humans who share their homes.

Let's face it, our cats run our households. We cater to their every feline food fancy: If they turn up their noses at dry food, we offer them canned and coax and plead with them to eat it. When the meal is over and after they've groomed themselves, we scratch them in that special place they love or we engage them with ten of their favorite toys. We exist to keep these beasts happy.

As cat owners who cater to the whims and fancies of our own cats, we've written this cookbook to help you treat your cat to an occasional special meal. Recipes included in this book are meant to be served as treats, not as regular meals. Nutrition experts say treats should comprise no more than 5 to 10 percent of your cat's diet. It's okay to indulge your favorite cat on special occasions, but don't overdo it. Your cat needs a complete and balanced diet formulated for its life stage. Control your cat's diet and you will be rewarded with a feline friend who will happily share your home for many years to come.

In addition to our treat recipes, we've provided a few basics about feline nutrition, as well as a brief overview of some illnesses that may affect your cat's eating habits. If your cat does exhibit any of the signs discussed, see your veterinarian immediately. If you're lucky enough to have a cat that requires only a yearly visit for a checkup and vaccinations, pat yourself on the back and keep up the good work.

Once your kitty has survived the traumatic car trip to and from the veterinarian's office, plan a special meal for it the following day—give your cat a day to recover from the car ride. Get your cat's favorite dish or your best silver tray and serve it something special.

In the following pages, you'll find fun recipes for holidays and birthdays, and a special section of our favorite recipes that are meant to be shared with your cat. We know you'll prepare these treats with a huge helping of love. And after Kitty has dined on a special treat, that favorite sleeping spot will be waiting. *Bon appétit* to you and your cat.

*Your Cat's
Nutritional Needs*

CHAPTER 1

Cats are the ultimate predators. They have sharp teeth and claws, powerful muscles, and bodies built for speed. You might say they are the high-performance race cars of the animal world. To fuel their engines, they need high-performance food: meat. Cats are *obligate carnivores*, which means that eating meat is biologically essential for their survival. This fact is indicated by the evolutionary development of the feline teeth and digestive system, which are specially designed to tear meat and then digest it quickly to provide the feline predator with the energy it needs.

Although dogs and cats both belong to the order *Carnivora*, meaning meat-eater, they have very different nutritional requirements. Cats require twice as much protein in their diets as dogs; and they have special needs for the amino acids arginine and taurine, as well as for vitamin A and arachidonic acid, all of which are available from meat.

Because of these dietary requirements, cats cannot thrive on a diet of dog food or table scraps. But neither can they live on meat or fish alone. The protein a cat needs must be balanced with the proper amounts of fats, carbohydrates, vitamins and minerals. Cats in the wild obtain these nutrients by eating the bones and stomach contents of their prey, but domestic cats must rely on their owners to provide complete and balanced meals.

That's why most veterinary nutritionists recommend that cats eat a complete, balanced, high-quality commercial food. Few owners are knowledgeable enough and dedicated enough to develop a proper diet and cook it themselves on a regular basis, especially in today's busy two-earner households. Cats love the taste of canned food, and dry food helps keep their teeth clean and tartar-free. Brand-name pet food manufacturers use ingredients that provide complete and balanced nutrition, and many test their foods' nutritional quality and palatability with feeding trials, in which a number of different types of cats are fed the diet to ensure that it meets their needs.

The recipes in the following chapters are special meals or treats your cat will enjoy. In many cases, the recipes are for meals that can be shared by you and your cat. To keep them special, and to prevent your cat from becoming finicky, serve homemade meals only occasionally. These recipes are not nutritionally complete, and they should make up no more than 5 to 10 percent of your cat's diet. Unless otherwise noted, servings should be limited to no more than $1/4$ cup.

Water: The Life-Giving Liquid

Cats can survive for days without food, but without water they will die quickly. That's not surprising, considering that 73 percent of an adult cat's body is made up of water. Along with its food, be sure your cat always has a supply of fresh, clean water. No other nutrient is as important to cats. Cells can't function without water, and water acts as a lubricant for tissues throughout the body. A number of bodily functions—and dysfunctions—eliminate water from the body, among them urination, defecation, lactation, respiration, panting, diarrhea and vomiting. That's why fluid replacement is especially important when a cat is sick.

In addition to regular water intake, the body absorbs water from food. As carbohydrates, fats and proteins are processed, they, too, contribute water. The amount of water a cat drinks depends on the type of food it eats. Because canned food contains a large amount of water, cats that eat primarily canned food tend to drink less water than those on a dry diet.

To safeguard his patients' health, one holistic veterinarian we know recommends that his clients give their pets filtered or bottled water. For a special treat, give your cat one of the many flavored bottled waters manufactured especially for pets.

Hint

If you take your cat on a cross-country trip or move to a new city, be sure to bring along a gallon or two of water from home. Mix the cat's regular water with the water in new areas to minimize digestive upsets.

Breakfast with Tiffany

CHAPTER 2

Bombay Kedgeree

Don't be surprised if your British Shorthair has an instinctive liking for kedgeree. Although this dish originated in India, it is a popular breakfast dish in Great Britain, which has historic ties to India.

1 cup cooked brown rice
³/₄ cup flaked smoked mackerel
¹/₄ cup chopped parsley
1 hard-boiled egg, chopped

In the 1950s, a cat breeder decided to create a black cat with copper eyes. She crossed a Burmese with a black American Shorthair, and after many generations of selective breeding, the Bombay was the result. This cat resembles a small black leopard and has a gentle, affectionate personality.

Combine all ingredients and mix well. Serve.

1 tablespoon butter

2 eggs, beaten

1/4 cup cottage cheese

Scottish Fold Scrambled Eggs

Scrambled eggs are healthy, as well as easy to fix. They take only two to three minutes to prepare and cook. Offer them to pique the appetite of a cat that isn't feeling well. Scrambled eggs are bland and smooth, and should sit well on an upset tummy.

Melt the butter in a frying pan, and remove from heat. Combine beaten eggs and cottage cheese, and pour into frying pan. Return pan to low heat, and stir the egg mixture with a fork until set. Serve separately or over the cat's regular food.

The Scottish Fold has small ears that fold forward and down, giving the cat an owl-like appearance. Cats with folded ears were first noted in China in 1796, but the breed as we know it today appeared in Scotland in 1961. Perhaps a long-ago Scottish sailor brought one of the unusual Chinese cats home with him.

Scrambled Eggs with Ham

1 egg
1 slice ham, finely chopped
2 tablespoons grated cheese
Splash of milk

Hint

Cats should always be fed cooked eggs, not raw, because raw egg whites interfere with the absorption of biotin, one of the B vitamins. Raw eggs also carry the danger of salmonella poisoning. Feed cooked eggs no more than twice a week.

Beat the egg; then add the chopped ham and grated cheese. Add a splash of milk (this makes scrambled eggs fluffy). Pour into skillet and gently scramble until thoroughly cooked. Cool to room temperature (takes about 10 minutes) and serve.

Place a small scoop (about 2 tablespoons) of cottage cheese in your cat's bowl. Top with cat-bite-size cubes of cantaloupe. This melon is a favorite among cats.

Cantaloupe with Cottage Cheese

"The Crumpet Cat is little known;
He sits him under trees,
And watches for the Muffin Bird
His palate for to please . . ."
—Laura E. Richards,
"The High Barbaree"

Meowsli

Many cats love fruit and yogurt, and will find this healthy cereal appealing. So will you!

1 tablespoon oats
$^1/_2$ **banana, mashed**
2 **tablespoons plain yogurt**
$^1/_2$ **cup orange juice**
$^1/_4$ **apple, chopped**
2 **ounces berries in season**

A descendant of the cats of ancient Egypt, the modern Egyptian Mau (the word "Mau" means cat, appropriately enough) was developed in Italy in 1953. Its spotted tabby coat comes in silver, bronze and smoke. The Mau is quick and curious, and likes to be involved in everything that is going on.

Mix oats and banana, blending well. Add yogurt, orange juice and apple immediately to prevent browning. Mash berries and add to mixture. Serve in small portions (1 tablespoon per cat); too much fruit can cause diarrhea in a digestive system that is not used to it.

Fruit and Yogurt

1 strawberry, chopped
1-inch piece banana, chopped
1 small chunk cantaloupe, chopped
1 tablespoon plain yogurt

Mix together and serve as a special summer treat for your cat.

11

Abyssinian Apple-Raisin Oatmeal

This makes a great winter morning breakfast for cats and people.

1 cup soy or rice milk

2 tablespoons brown sugar

1½ teaspoons butter

⅛ teaspoon salt

⅛ teaspoon cinnamon

½ cup rolled oats

½ cup chopped apple

¼ cup raisins

Another breed with a long history, the Abyssinian is believed to be descended from the cats of ancient Egypt. It was brought to Europe from Abyssinia (present-day Ethiopia) in the mid-nineteenth century. Today it is a popular breed with a lively, curious personality. This is a bright cat that demands constant attention and requires close supervision to prevent it from dismantling the household.

Preheat oven to 350° F. Combine milk, brown sugar, butter, salt and cinnamon in an ovenproof pot and bring to a boil. Remove pot from heat and stir in oats, apple and raisins. Bring mixture to a simmer, place pot in oven and cook uncovered for 8 to 10 minutes. Remove from oven, let cool and serve.

Kitty Flakes

Prepare your favorite bowl of breakfast cereal, topped with milk, of course. Sit down at the breakfast table with the morning paper, and invite your cat to join you on your lap (not that most cats need an invitation). When you're finished eating, offer your cat the mushy milk and cereal remains. (Don't forget that some cats are lactose intolerant. Too much milk can cause them to throw up, but generally small amounts can be tolerated.)

Tabby Appeteasers

C H A P T E R   3

Breath Biscuits

2 cups brown rice flour
1 tablespoon activated charcoal (can
   be purchased at the drugstore)
1 large egg, lightly beaten
3 tablespoons vegetable oil
$^1/_2$ cup chopped parsley
$^1/_3$ cup chopped fresh mint
$^2/_3$ cup milk

Could your cat's breath knock Arnold Schwarzenegger flat? Try sweetening it with these biscuits, which contain charcoal, parsley and mint to fight bad breath. The hard texture will help remove tartar buildup.

Preheat oven to 400° F. Grease baking sheet. Combine flour and charcoal. In another bowl, combine the egg, oil, parsley and mint, and mix well. Gradually stir in the flour mixture, and add enough of the milk to make a dough the consistency of drop biscuits. Drop heaping teaspoons of dough onto the baking sheet about one inch apart. Bake 15 minutes, or until firm. Store the cooled biscuits in a tightly covered container in the refrigerator.

Hint

To keep your cat's teeth really clean, brush them two to three times a week and schedule annual veterinary dental cleanings. Toothbrushes and toothpaste made specially for cats are available from your veterinarian or from a pet supply store. Don't brush Smoky's teeth with a toothpaste formulated for people. The ingredients can cause stomach upset.

15

Somali Sausage Biscuit Bites

1 pound sharp cheddar cheese, grated
1 pound mild turkey sausage, crumbled
3 cups dry biscuit baking mix

This is yet another breed whose name has nothing to do with its place of origin. The Somali is the longhaired sibling of the Abyssinian and first appeared in Abyssinian litters in the United States. It is an independent but affectionate cat that is not quite as "busy" and mischievous as the Abyssinian.

Preheat oven to 400° F. Combine cheese and sausage in a saucepan; heat and stir until cheese is melted. Add biscuit mix, and stir until smooth. Let mixture cool until easy to handle. Shape into small balls, and place on ungreased baking sheet. Bake for 8 to 10 minutes. Remove from oven, and drain on paper towels. Serve at room temperature. Refrigerate to store.

1 pound chicken livers
1 hard-boiled egg
1/4 cup chopped apple

Mancattan Chopped Chicken Liver

Give your cat a taste of the Big Apple. This is a fast, easy microwave recipe.

Remove connective tissues from chicken livers and rinse. Place livers in a single layer on a microwave-safe dish, and cover tightly with microwave-safe plastic wrap. Microwave on high for 2 to 3 minutes. Uncover and stir; replace plastic wrap and microwave on high for 3 minutes. Put livers in food processor, add egg and apple, and chop coarsely. Serve.

*"Taffy, the topaz-coloured cat,
Thinks now of this and now of that,
But chiefly of his meals.
Asparagus, and cream, and fish,
Are objects of his Freudian wish;
What you don't give, he steals."*
—Christopher Morley,
"In Honor of Taffy Topaz"

Savory Salmon Patties

1 egg, beaten
4 to 6 plain crackers, crushed
1 6-ounce can boneless, skinless
   salmon, drained

Hint

Groom your cat weekly if it has short hair, as often as daily if it has long hair. Using a brush or comb, go over your cat's body to remove loose hair. This ounce of prevention can mean fewer hairballs. At the end of the grooming session, reward your cat with a treat.

Preheat oven to 325° F. Beat the egg, then add crackers and mix. Add salmon, and mix. Shape into small patties and bake for 20 minutes. Cool to room temperature and serve. Baked patties may be frozen, then thawed, reheated and served.

Fine Fish and Seafood

CHAPTER 4

Supurrr Salmon Pâté

1 6-ounce can boneless, skinless
   salmon
$1/4$ cup bread crumbs
$1/2$ cup finely chopped celery
1 egg, beaten
1 envelope unflavored gelatin
$1/2$ cup water

Hint

Real cats don't eat sushi. Avoid giving your cat raw fish. Not only may it contain parasites, it can also cause a thiamine deficiency, indicated by appetite loss, weakness and seizures. Unless its diet is corrected, a cat with a thiamine deficiency can die.

Preheat oven to 325° F. Combine all ingredients and mix well. Pack into a small fish-shaped mold and bake for 45 minutes. Serve at room temperature.

1 cup cooked salad shrimp
1 hard-boiled egg, finely chopped

Balinese Shrimp Salad

Combine shrimp and egg and mix well.
Serve separately or with dry cat food.

The graceful Balinese did not originate on the island of Bali; it first appeared as a mutation in litters of Siamese kittens in the 1950s. It resembles a longhaired Siamese but is a distinct breed.

21

Turkey of the Sea

4 ounces cod fillets

1 egg

1 teaspoon oregano

dry bread crumbs

2 tablespoons butter

½ cup lactose-free milk or rice milk

2 new potatoes, quartered, boiled and
mashed

Hint

Feeding a wide variety of complete and balanced foods appropriate for your cat's stage of life is the best way to ensure that it gets the nutrients it needs.

Cut fillets into 1-inch cubes. Combine egg and oregano, and mix well. Dip pieces of cod into egg mixture and then into crumbs. Heat butter in saucepan, and brown cod until golden. Add milk and simmer over low heat for about 10 minutes. Mix cod with potatoes and serve at room temperature.

1 cup canned low-sodium chicken broth
1/2 cup instant brown rice, uncooked
1/2 teaspoon oregano
3/4 cup chopped green beans
1 6-ounce can tuna
1 hard-boiled egg, chopped

Tuna-Rice Chartreux

This recipe is based on France's famous Nicoise salad, which contains several favorite feline ingredients: tuna, egg and green beans. Cats can become addicted to tuna, so serve this dish only rarely.

Bring broth to a boil, then add rice, oregano and green beans. Reduce heat, cover, and simmer for 10 minutes or until rice is done. Add tuna and egg, and mix well. Serve at room temperature.

The Chartreux, a French breed, has been described as looking like a potato on toothpicks. This handsome gray cat has striking orange eyes.

23

Fried Catfish

The catfish takes its name from the long whiskers that frame its face.

8 ounces catfish fillets (be sure to check for bones), cut into nuggets
Buttermilk
Cornmeal
2 tablespoons butter

Did you know? Cats come in more than seventy-five colors, combinations of colors, and patterns. Among them are agouti, a tabby pattern in which the hairs consist of two or three bands of color; lavender, a pinkish-gray color; and mackerel tabby, a pattern consisting of thin, sharply contrasting stripes, an intricate "M" design on the forehead, a ringed tail, and a double row of spots that run down the chest to the stomach.

Soak catfish nuggets in buttermilk for about 15 minutes. Drain buttermilk, then dredge catfish in cornmeal, coating well. Fry in butter until golden-brown. Cool to room temperature and serve. Makes four servings.

Pasta with Clam Sauce

1 cup small macaroni or orzo (rice-shaped pasta), uncooked

1 tablespoon olive oil

1 10-ounce can clams, drained

1 14-ounce can tomatoes, chopped

2 tablespoons parsley, chopped

Cook pasta according to package directions. While pasta is cooking, heat olive oil in a skillet and add clams, tomatoes and 1 tablespoon of the parsley. Heat well. When pasta is done, drain the water and add the pasta to the clam sauce. Let cool to room temperature and serve. Top with remaining parsley; many cats enjoy this herb. Serving size: $1/4$ cup.

"Mr. Leonard, a very intelligent friend of mine, saw a cat catch a trout, by darting upon it in a deep clear water, at the mill at Weaford, near Lichfield. The cat belonged to Mr. Stanley, who had often seen her catch fish in the same manner in summer, when the mill-pool was drawn so low that the fish could be seen. I have heard of other cats taking fish in shallow water, as they stood on the bank. This seems to be a natural method of taking their prey, usually lost by domestication, though they all retain a strong relish for fish."

—Charles Darwin

Savory Soups and Stews

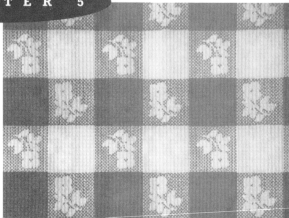

CHAPTER 5

1 cup homemade chicken stock or
   canned low-sodium chicken
   broth

2 eggs

1/2 cup slivered cooked chicken

Pour chicken stock into a saucepan and bring to a simmer. While stock is heating, beat eggs in a small bowl. When stock is hot, add about 1/4 cup to beaten eggs, stirring continuously. Slowly add egg-stock mixture to the rest of the stock, stirring continuously. Add chicken and stir well. Pour soup into one large bowl or four small custard cups and cover with foil. Place containers on the rack of a steamer set over simmering water, and steam for 20 to 30 minutes, until done. Cool to room temperature and serve.

Oriental Chicken Custard

Chicken soup cures just about anything, according to grandmothers everywhere. This soothing dish may comfort a cat that's not feeling well.

Like the Siamese, the Oriental Shorthair originated in Thailand. It is a Siamese in all but appearance: Its coat lacks the characteristic point markings of the Siamese. It is an adaptable, companionable cat, unusual in that it is amenable to leash-training.

Chicken Poodle Soup

Our cats were really excited when we served this because they thought it contained real poodle. We didn't disabuse them of the notion. Shelby and Peter especially liked it served over dry cat food.

1 chicken drumstick
1 cup water
pinch of salt
2 tablespoons frozen mixed
   vegetables

Hint

Do not feed any of these meals in excess. Use common sense in deciding how often to feed a homemade treat or meal and how much to serve your cat. One or two tablespoons served with its regular food is an adequate amount for the average-size cat.

In a small saucepan, slowly bring the chicken leg to a boil in the water. Add salt, and cook slowly until chicken is done. Remove the chicken leg from the liquid, reserving the broth. Remove the meat from the bone and discard the skin. Cut the meat into small, cat-bite-size pieces. Return the chicken pieces to the broth and add the vegetables. Heat thoroughly. Remove from heat and let soup cool for about 10 minutes. Serve to Kitty. Makes three to four cat servings.

1 cup nonfat, low-sodium chicken
   broth
3 to 4 large shrimp, cooked, peeled,
   deveined and chopped
$^1/_2$ small potato, peeled, boiled and cut
   into cat-bite-size chunks

Shrimp and Potato Soup

Combine ingredients, heat and serve.

Hint

To give a pill, kneel on the floor and place your cat's back between your legs. Gently tilt your cat's head back, open its mouth and place the pill on the back of the cat's tongue. Hold the cat's mouth closed and stroke its throat until it swallows. You may also hide the pill in a treat, such as cream cheese or peanut butter.

Shrimp Soup

3 to 4 large shrimp, peeled and
    deveined
1 cup water
$1/4$ cup small cooked pasta, such as
    orzo, or cooked rice

Cook the shrimp in the water; when cooked, remove shrimp from water and reserve the liquid. Chop shrimp into cat-bite-size pieces, and return to broth. Add cooked rice or pasta. Serve at room temperature. Makes two servings for a single-cat household.

1 avocado, mashed
1 can cream of chicken soup
½ cup plain yogurt or tofu
1 cup water

Chicken-Avocado Soup

This is a refreshing pick-me-up on a hot day. You and your cat will both enjoy it.

Place all ingredients in blender or food processor and mix well. Serve. (You may prefer your portion chilled.)

Hint

If your cat urinates or defecates outside its litter box, it may have a serious medical problem. Take the cat to your veterinarian right away to rule out any physical problems. Once these have been ruled out, concentrate on correcting your cat's behavior. Ask your veterinarian to refer you to a behaviorist.

British Blue Beefy Vegetable Stew

1 tablespoon olive oil
1 pound stew beef, in 1-inch cubes
1 can sodium-free beef broth
1 cup water
1 teaspoon oregano
8-ounce can diced tomatoes, with
    liquid
1 can kidney beans, undrained
1 cup mixed vegetables
$^1/_2$ cup small macaroni

The British Shorthair is a powerful yet compact cat that is known for being an able hunter. The solid blue British Shorthair is extremely popular, and this coat color is considered typical of the breed. The British Shorthair may also come in other solid colors, as well as tabby, smoke, parti-color, dilute and bicolor patterns.

Heat olive oil in pan. Brown beef. Add broth, water and oregano, and simmer for 1 hour. Add tomatoes, beans, mixed vegetables and macaroni, and simmer for another 45 minutes. Serve at room temperature.

1 1/2 teaspoons olive oil

1 pound ground lamb

1 carrot, peeled and diced

1 small zucchini, peeled and diced

1 8-ounce can diced tomatoes

3/4 cup water

1/2 cup couscous

1/4 cup lactose-free milk

Persian Lamb Stew

Heat oil in a large skillet and brown lamb for 10 to 12 minutes. Add carrot, zucchini, tomatoes and water. Bring to a boil; then reduce heat, cover and simmer until lamb is tender, about 1 to 1 1/4 hours. Add more water if necessary to prevent scorching. When the lamb is done, prepare the couscous according to package directions. Mix couscous with lamb stew, and serve at room temperature.

The Persian is one of the oldest of breeds and first appeared around 1520 in Europe, where it was probably brought from Persia or Turkey. Its long, full coat of many colors, which can grow to six or eight inches, is this cat's crowning glory.

33

*Meat Meals Your Cat
Will Meow For*

CHAPTER 6

1 pound extra-lean ground beef

¹/₄ cup chopped fresh parsley

1 egg

2 tablespoons ketchup

¹/₂ cup dry bread crumbs

¹/₄ teaspoon garlic powder

Manx Meatballs

Preheat oven to 450° F. Combine all ingredients in a large bowl and mix well. Shape into small balls, and place on broiler pan rack. Bake until brown, 10 to 15 minutes. Serve at room temperature. Refrigerate to store.

This tailless cat hails from the Isle of Man, from which it takes its name. It is said that Manx cats lost their tails when they arrived late to Noah's ark. Just as the cats jumped aboard, Noah slammed the door—right on their tails! The Manx also comes in a longhaired version called the Cymric.

Cornish Rex Steak and Kidney Pie

1/2 cup diced kidney fat
1 beef kidney, trimmed of fat and
    diced
1 pound stew beef, diced
3 cups hot water
1/2 cup flour, browned
1/2 cup cold water
pastry for 2-crust pie

The Rex breeds (Cornish, Devon and Selkirk) are distinguished by their curly coats. Even their whiskers are curly.

Melt kidney fat in saucepan, and add diced kidney and beef. Brown over high heat for 2 minutes. Add hot water and bring to a boil. Cover and simmer until meat is tender. Make a paste by stirring browned flour into cold water. Stir into stew until thickened. Line pie plate or casserole dish with pastry, and top with stew. Cover with second crust. Be sure to prick the top so the steam can escape. Bake at 400° F. until crust is brown. Let cool and serve.

1 lean, boneless pork chop

¾ cup water

2 small slices of apple, peeled and
    cored

Lick Your Chops Pork Chops

Your cat may find these pork chops with apples a whisker-licking-good treat.

Bring the meat to a boil in the water. Add apples. Let simmer for about 15 minutes. Remove meat and apples from water. Chop into fine pieces, or process in food processor. Serve at room temperature.

A cat has about a dozen whiskers on each side of its face, usually arranged in four horizontal rows.

Ten o'Clock—Crazies Chicken Salad

1 5-ounce can chunk boneless white chicken
2 tablespoons plain yogurt
1 teaspoon celery, finely chopped
4 seedless grapes, finely chopped

Playing with your cat every day is one of the many ways you can express your love for your pet. Engaging your cat in play with a toy will keep your cat active and fit. And the two of you will look forward to many fun-filled play sessions. When the session is over, be sure to store any toys with long strings in locations not accessible to your cat. Your cat could become dangerously entangled in toys with long strings, or it could ingest string, if it is left unsupervised.

Combine all ingredients, making sure chicken is cut into small pieces. Mix and serve. Leftovers can be refrigerated.

1 tablespoon olive oil

½ cup brown rice

1 clove garlic, chopped

1 cup diced tomatoes

1 cup water or low-sodium chicken broth

1 cup chicken, cubed

Chessie's Chicken and Rice

This is a favorite of both humans and animals in our household.

Heat olive oil in skillet and add rice and garlic. Brown for 5 minutes. Add tomatoes, water and chicken, stir and cover. Simmer for 30 minutes, or until rice is tender. Serve at room temperature. Makes four servings.

The symbol of the Chesapeake Railroad was a tabby kitten named Chessie, shown in advertisements sleeping in an air-conditioned Pullman car.

39

Down and Dirty Rice

Cats that live in the South may already be accustomed to this delicacy, but Yankee cats are sure to enjoy it, too. Feed liver dishes no more than once a week. Liver is high in vitamin A, which builds up quickly in the body and can cause toxicity.

Hint

If your cat is eating a complete and balanced commercial diet, it does not need vitamin or mineral supplements. Too many vitamins and minerals can cause just as much harm as too few. Veterinarians usually recommend supplements only for cats that eat homemade diets, cats that are diagnosed with deficiencies, older cats, and pregnant or lactating cats.

4 ounces chopped chicken gizzards

4 ounces chopped chicken livers

1 celery rib, finely chopped, or ¹/₂ cup finely chopped green beans

1 tablespoon canola oil

¹/₂ cup instant brown rice, uncooked

1 cup chicken broth

¹/₄ cup chopped parsley

Chop gizzards, livers and celery or green beans in food processor. Heat oil in skillet and add meat mixture, browning for about 10 minutes. Add rice, and stir. Add broth and bring to a boil, stirring to get up any ingredients that may have stuck to the pan. Reduce heat, and cook for 10 minutes or until rice is done. Top with parsley and serve at room temperature. Makes two full servings or a number of tablespoon-size appetizer servings. Refrigerate or freeze leftovers. (Freeze in an ice cube tray for easy single servings. Simply pop out, thaw and serve.)

2 cups water

3 boneless, skinless chicken breasts

1 can cream of chicken soup

1 stick margarine, melted

1 cup self-rising flour

1 cup buttermilk

$1/2$ teaspoon black pepper

Bring the water to a boil in a saucepan, and add the two chicken breasts. Reduce heat and allow chicken to cook slowly. When done, remove chicken breasts from water; reserve broth. Cut breasts into small pieces and return to broth. (This step can be done in advance, and the chicken and broth frozen.) Add cream of chicken soup to broth and chicken, and heat. In a separate bowl, combine the melted margarine, flour, buttermilk and pepper, and mix well. Spoon the warmed chicken mixture into two 2-quart casserole dishes, and spoon the batter over the chicken mixture. Bake in a 375° F. oven for 25 to 30 minutes.

Moscow's Chicken Pot Pie

Reprinted with permission from the *Winston-Salem Journal*

Hint

Take your cat to the veterinarian for a yearly physical examination and vaccinations. To prepare for the visit, write down any questions you want to ask your cat's doctor. If you are visiting a new veterinarian, be sure to take your cat's previous veterinary records.

Nutty Siamese Stirfry

Believe it or not, many cats love the taste of peanut butter. They will relish this chicken dish topped with a Thai peanut sauce.

$^1/_4$ cup smooth peanut butter made with peanuts only, no sugar or salt
1 tablespoon water
2 tablespoons butter
1 chicken breast, cut into nuggets

The Siamese is one of the most recognizable and popular of the cat breeds. It came from Siam (present-day Thailand), where it dates to the fourteenth century or earlier. Like the Abyssinian, the Siamese is an active, demanding cat that requires an understanding and attentive owner.

Combine peanut butter and water in blender or food processor, and process until smooth. Melt butter in skillet and stirfry chicken until done, about 2 minutes on each side. Top with peanut sauce; let cool to room temperature and serve.

1 egg, beaten

2 tablespoons milk

1 pound chicken, diced into nuggets

1/2 cup plain dry bread crumbs

1/2 cup grated Parmesan cheese

1 tablespoon oregano

Ocicat Oregano Chicken

Preheat oven to 350° F. Combine egg and milk, and mix well. Pour over chicken nuggets. In a separate bowl, combine bread crumbs, Parmesan and oregano. Remove chicken pieces from egg-milk mixture and dredge in crumb mixture. Repeat if necessary to coat chicken well. Place chicken on greased baking sheet, and bake about 40 minutes, or until coating is crisp.

The striking spotted Ocicat has Siamese, Abyssinian and American Shorthair in its ancestry. Not surprisingly, this cat is lively and athletic, always looking for a good time.

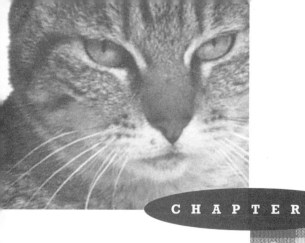

Feline Feasts

CHAPTER 7

NEW YEAR'S

DAY

Hoppin' John

Ensure your cat a healthy, prosperous year by feeding this Southern good-luck dish first thing on New Year's Day. It should be the first thing you eat, too!

2 strips bacon

1 can black-eyed peas, drained and rinsed, or 1 10-ounce package frozen black-eyed peas

$\frac{1}{2}$ cup long-grain rice, uncooked

1 cup water

Dice bacon and fry in skillet. Add peas, rice and water. Cover and simmer over low heat for 20 to 25 minutes, or until rice is done. Cool and serve.

ST. PATRICK'S DAY

For St. Patrick's Day, you may wish to treat your cat to some greens—grass and catnip, that is. Both of these can be grown in a sunny windowsill or in an herb garden.

For reasons unknown to experts, cats like to eat grass. Some feline nutritionists believe cats eat grass because they are missing certain nutrients and en-

zymes from their diets; others think cats nibble on this green stuff to help them get rid of hairballs. Whatever the reason, cats enjoy grazing on a nice patch of grass.

A few stalks of fresh catnip from your garden will make a cat roll, rub, frolic and play as it enjoys the high from this plant. Cats experience catnip through a unique sense that is a combination of taste and smell. The smell of catnip is received through the vomeronasal, or Jacobson's, organ, located in the roof of a cat's mouth. What follows is a wonderfully intoxicating "catnip trip." But not all cats respond to catnip, and this herb should not be given to kittens under six months of age.

If you grow catnip indoors, be sure the pots are placed away from your cat's reach, or the plants may be harvested at will by a feline gardener. Don't spray this plant with any chemicals or pesticides.

Catnip can be enjoyed by humans, too—though not in quite the same way cats go crazy for it. Catnip leaves may be used to make tea, which can be used as a sleeping aid.

APRIL FOOL'S DAY

No Fool Pie*

When Jane's cat Moscow gets a chance, she licks clean the plate that contains this dessert.

*From Red Band Flour.

³/₄ stick butter or margarine

1 cup self-rising flour

³/₄ cup sugar

³/₄ cup milk

1 to 1¹/₂ cups fruit (blueberries or peaches are good)

Preheat oven to 350° F. While oven is heating, melt margarine in an 8- or 9-inch baking dish. Set aside. Combine flour, sugar and half the milk. Stir until dry ingredients are moistened. Add remaining milk; stir until smooth. Pour batter over melted margarine, but do not mix. Top with drained fruit, but do not stir to combine. Bake 30 to 40 minutes until lightly browned. Serve warm. Reheats well in microwave.

"O my Enemy and Wife of my Enemy and Mother of my Enemy," said the cat, ". . . you have spoken three words in my praise, and now I can drink the warm white milk three times a day for always and always and always. But still I am the Cat who walks by himself, and all places are alike to me." Then the woman laughed and set the Cat a bowl of the warm white milk and said "O Cat, you are as clever as a man."

—Rudyard Kipling,
"The Cat That Walked by Himself"

INDEPENDENCE

DAY

Fran Greene's Blueberry Salad

Moscow especially likes the topping for this salad.

2 packages black raspberry gelatin
    dessert mix
2³⁄₄ cups hot water
1 can blueberries, drained
1 can pineapple, drained (be sure to
    drain the pineapple well, or the
    salad will not congeal)
1 8-ounce package cream cheese
¹⁄₂ cup sugar
¹⁄₂ pint sour cream
¹⁄₂ teaspoon vanilla

Combine gelatin mix and hot water. Place in refrigerator. When slightly congealed, fold in the drained fruit. Allow salad to congeal. To make topping, combine cream cheese, sugar, sour cream and vanilla. Mix well and pour over the top of the congealed salad. Chill for several hours before serving.

FOURTH OF JULY

If you let your cat go outdoors, be sure to keep it in on the Fourth of July. The noise of fireworks can scare cats, and they may run away from home and get lost.

HALLOWEEN

1 sweet potato
2 tablespoons butter
2 tablespoons brown sugar

Sweet Potato Tricky Treat

Cook the sweet potato in water, then peel it. Cut the potato into small pieces and mash up. Mix in the other ingredients, then bake in a dish for about 10 minutes at 375°. Cool to room temperature and serve. Makes 4 servings for a single-cat household.

Black cats have long been a symbol for Halloween, but many cat lovers believe black cats bring good luck. No matter what color your cat is, be sure to keep it inside during the celebration for All Hallows' Eve. You may want to sequester your cat in its favorite room so that it doesn't escape during one of the many times through the night that the door is opened for little ghosts and goblins collecting candy.

THANKSGIVING

What a wonderful time of year to acknowledge how much cats enrich our lives. It's okay to give your cat a special Thanksgiving treat, but offer only one treat and don't overindulge your cat. Kindly remind your guests, too, not to overfeed Kitty.

Your feline friend may enjoy a tiny amount of cooked turkey with a few drops of gravy, or you may wish to prepare the turkey's gizzard and liver for your cat. (These can be found inside your turkey; they're the items everyone is always reminding you to remove before baking the bird.) To do so, thoroughly wash the liver and gizzard, and place them in about 1 cup of water. Bring to a boil, then reduce heat and simmer for 15–20 minutes until thoroughly cooked. Chop, and serve to your cat.

Don't give the cat the turkey carcass to scavenge. A bone could become lodged in your cat's throat or stomach, requiring a trip to the veterinary emergency room.

Tonkinese Turkey Loaf

1 pound ground turkey, crumbled
8 crackers, crumbled, or $^1/_2$ cup plain
    bread crumbs
2 tablespoons carrot, finely chopped
1 egg
4 ounces tomato sauce

Preheat oven to 325° F. Mix all ingredients in a bowl. Form into two loaves. Bake for 40 minutes. Once the turkey loaf has cooled, slice into portions appropriate to your cat household. Individual slices may be frozen, then thawed and reheated for a treat.

CHRISTMAS

Oyster Stew

Oysters are a traditional part of the holiday feast, and cats love them too. You might serve this stew on Christmas Eve.

2 tablespoons butter

1/2 cup celery

1 pint oysters with liquor

1 1/2 cups milk

1/2 cup cream

1/8 teaspoon paprika

2 tablespoons chopped parsley

"I shall never forget the indulgence with which Dr. Johnson treated Hodge, his cat; for whom he himself used to go out and buy oysters . . ."
—James Boswell, The Life of Samuel Johnson

Tip: A special holiday gift for your cat might include a new collar (be sure it's one that will break away if it gets hung up on something) and identification tag. Even if your cat never ventures outside, it is a good idea for him to wear identification should he slip out the door.

Over direct heat, melt the butter in the top of a double boiler and sauté the celery for 5 minutes. Add oysters, milk, cream and paprika, and place the pot over boiling water. Cook until the milk is hot and the oysters float. Top with parsley. Let cool before serving to your cat.

YOUR CAT'S
BIRTHDAY

Birthday Treat

1 to 2 ounces poached fish, preferably
   salmon, with the skin and bones
   removed
1 teaspoon plain yogurt
Few drops of fresh lemon juice

Hint

Poach the fish. Then mix the yogurt and lemon juice and serve over the cooked fish.

Your cat's birthday is a good time to check the calendar to be sure it is current on vaccinations and its annual physical examination by your veterinarian. Scheduling your cat's veterinary visit close to its birthday is a good way to keep track of when your cat is due for a checkup.

Another way to honor your cat on its birthday would be to make a donation in your cat's name to a local animal shelter; or to the veterinary school in your state, to be used toward the study of feline medicine.

1 pound ground turkey
1 egg (or 2 egg whites)
3/4 cup oatmeal
1/8 teaspoon garlic powder
1/4 cup minced parsley
Nonfat cream cheese

Birthday Cake

If you don't know when your cat's birthday is, celebrate on the day you adopted it or choose some other date that has special meaning—your own birthday, for instance. That way, the two of you can celebrate together.

Preheat oven to 350° F. Mix turkey, eggs, oatmeal, garlic powder and parsley thoroughly, and mold into desired shape. You can go with the traditional round or square look, or create a fish, bird or mouse shape. Bake on a broiler pan or on a rack over a cookie sheet for 30 to 45 minutes, until done. Remove from the oven and let cool. Frost with tinted lowfat cream cheese. If you want to serve individual "cupcakes," cut out shapes with a cookie cutter before baking.

"They dined on mince, and slices of quince,
Which they ate with a runcible spoon . . ."

—Edward Lear,
"The Owl and the Pussycat"

Tricks for Treats

Your feline friend is probably more intelligent than you give it credit for. Scientific literature suggests that cats are smart—you just have to find them the right reward for demonstrating their intelligence.

Cats have a different social system than dogs, and they learn in different ways than dogs. A cat will find a tasty treat a better reward than a scratch behind the ears, a reward considered acceptable by a dog. "Having a really tasty treat, something that really gets a cat's attention—that's what you want," says Dan Estep, Ph.D., an animal behaviorist.

Moscow, who is fifteen years old, knows what time her owner needs to get up in the morning—when Moscow's ready to eat. At feline breakfast time, Moscow jumps back and forth over Jane, then begins pawing at her ear. When all else fails, she nips the end of Jane's nose. When Jane can't take it any more and gives up trying to go back to sleep, she gets up and feeds Moscow.

Your cat may know mealtime is coming when it hears the cabinet or refrigerator open, or the whir of the can opener. A cat you thought was sleeping suddenly appears, racing at breakneck speed for the food dish.

In Moscow's case, the cat has trained the human; in the latter example, the human has trained the cat. Both are examples of conditioned response: Cats know that if they can wake their humans, the two-legged creatures will put food in dishes for the four-legged beings. When humans regularly use the electrical device that makes a whirring sound, they can count on their cats appearing for meals. It's all about training.

But wouldn't you like for your cat to use its training to your advantage? Teaching a cat to perform tricks can be fun and rewarding for friends and family.

Time spent with your cat will stimulate it and strengthen the relationship you and your cat share.

The key to effective training is consistency, says Karen Thomas, an animal trainer for Critters of the Cinema. Karen is one of the Friskies Cat Team trainers and has trained animals that have appeared in "Beverly Hills 90210," "Murder, She Wrote," "Demon Knight" and "Star Trek: The Next Generation."

Schedule a time to train your cat twice a day, and stick to your plan. Follow the same routine during each training session, and use the same methods and equipment. Be sure to give your cat plenty of praise and affection. You may also want to have your cat examined by a veterinarian before training begins, just as humans should have a physical exam before beginning an exercise program. Also, consider your cat's age and temperament when deciding what tricks to try teaching it. Younger, more active cats may be better suited to jumping than older cats.

Once you've made a training plan, gather a few supplies for your training toolbox: a toy clicker, tasty cat treats, any props for special tricks, and a healthy dose of patience. Set up a table to be used for training sessions; it's easier to train a cat on your level rather than bending to a cat's. Clear the table of all items.

The goal is to teach your cat to perform a certain behavior when it hears a specific sound—the clicker—just like when your cat runs to the kitchen after it hears the can opener. This is called a conditioned response. To get your cat to respond during training, attach a toy clicker to a spoon, or hold the clicker in one hand and the treat in the other. When the cat performs the behavior being taught, press the clicker and give the cat the treat.

Sound simple enough? You're ready to begin training.

Train your cat at the same time each day, and plan to spend five to ten minutes twice a day as you begin a training routine. Cats have a short attention span, so stop the session before the cat becomes bored, tired or angry. Trainers suggest that these sessions should take place before breakfast and dinner times, when your cat is feeling hungry. Start your training session with a couple of easy tricks: Sit and Lie Down.

Sit

To begin, place your cat on the table. Raise the treat over the cat's head. As the cat looks up, it will sit. As soon as your cat sits, click the clicker and give the treat. The key is to click when the cat performs the right behavior so it knows what the reward is given for. Thomas urges cat owners not to become dis-couraged during early training attempts. Use short sessions and be consistent. Perseverance pays off; cats and owners will both learn during the training process. In addition to learning, the time spent training is a healthy way to keep your cat from becoming bored and wanting to spend the day shredding the sofa. The stimulation that training provides gives your cat something about which to be excited.

This trick also comes in handy when photographing your cat. When your cat masters this trick, get out the camera and take great snapshots of your cat posing for the lens. Be sure to share them with all your cat-loving friends and brag about how your cat is trained to sit on command.

Lie Down

Once your cat learns to sit, try teaching it to lie down. To begin, place the cat on the table. With one hand, lower the clicker to the edge of the table. Then take your other hand and gently guide your cat to a prone position. Click the clicker and reward the cat with food.

Beyond sitting and lying down, the sky's the limit for teaching a cat tricks. You can also teach your cat to sit up and beg, roll over, speak and wave by using a conditioned response. For an advanced trick, teach your feline friend to jump through a hoop. This trick will certainly impress guests at your next dinner party. Think of the fun your guests will have when you present your own troupe of feline performers.

Hoop Da Loop

You'll need a hoop to teach your cat this trick. Professional trainers suggest a plastic hoop, such as a hula hoop that has been cut down to a manageable

size. Decorating the hoop with ribbon can add some color to this routine.

Place your cat on the training table and hold the hoop up, resting the bottom of the hoop on the table. This trick should be taught in several parts: First, have your cat walk through the hoop. When it walks through the hoop, click the clicker and reward it with a treat. Once your cat has learned to walk through the hoop, slowly raise the hoop about an inch at a time over several weeks. Each time your cat walks or jumps through the hoop, click and reward it with food. If your cat is hesitant about jumping through the hoop at a certain height, keep it below that height until your cat becomes comfortable. As your cat learns to jump through the hoop when it's raised, be sure there is enough room on the table for the cat to take a few steps before jumping through the hoop and then to take a few more steps after it lands. Thomas uses a six-foot-long banquet table as her training area. Don't reward your cat for going around the hoop. You will only encourage him to perform incorrectly.

When you begin training, stick with one trick until you and your cat get the hang of it. As soon as you are both comfortable performing that trick, add another one to the cat's routine. You can teach a cat several tricks at the same time, as long as the tricks involve different types of behaviors. For instance, don't teach a cat to wave and give you five, trainers advise. Instead, teach your cat two different tricks, such as to wave and roll over.

Always end each training session on a positive note. Never punish your cat during a session; save corrections for something serious, like scratching the couch. Instead, give your cat lots of love and scratches, as well as treats, when it performs the required behavior.

High Degree of Difficulty

Now that your favorite cat has mastered the basics, you may want to try something more challenging. Your cat may do some cute thing just for you, such as sitting on your shoulder kneading your hair, that you would like to teach it to perform on command.

The most difficult tricks to teach cats for movies or television are natural behaviors, such as stalking or kneading. Cats don't realize what they're doing, so to train them to perform a natural behavior on cue requires waiting for them to perform it so you can click and reward with food. You can teach your cat to show these skills, but it requires a lot of patience and training.

Tricks Our Cats Know

Moscow has a trick called Show Me Your Paw. To perform this trick, Moscow must already be in the "ready" position: sitting on the floor paying attention to every word Jane says. Jane leans over to tell Moscow what a wonderful cat she is and how much she is loved. When the two make eye contact, Jane says in a high-pitched voice, "Show me your paw." Moscow will lean slightly to the right and raise her left front paw. Then, with a gleeful meow, she holds the pose and waits for her reward, a nice scratch between the ears and a treat.

This trick should not be confused with the dog version, Shake, because Moscow just shows her paw. She's not too keen on shaking with it. Save that part for Rover.

Whistle Signal

Kim's three cats, Shelby, Peter and Pandora, come to a specific whistle. Most people think only dogs can be trained to come to a whistle, but it's very easy to teach your cat this trick, too. Merely associate the whistle with something pleasant, such as mealtime. It's as simple as preparing your cat's food. As you set the dish down, whistle a tune. Repeat this with each meal, and soon your cat will come running when it hears that special call. This comes in handy when you need to find the cat in a hurry. Don't use the whistle to call your cat for something unpleasant, such as a bath or a trip to the veterinarian, or your cat will soon unlearn it!

Is Your Cat Fat?

CHAPTER 9

We all know a fat cat. He waddles when he walks—if he walks—and food is what he lives for. The sound of the can opener or the rattle of a bag is the only thing that will get this cat moving. Veterinarians report that as many as 25 percent of the cats they see in their practices are obese. That means they weigh 10 percent or more over their ideal weight. To tell if your cat weighs too much, take the following quiz:

When Thumper hears the can opener in action,
a. The dishes rattle as he comes thundering into the kitchen.
b. He meows piteously, waiting anxiously for you to bring his food dish to him, because he's too slow and lazy to walk to the kitchen.
c. He purrs appreciatively while you fix his meal, eats some of it to satisfy his current appetite, and saves the rest for later.

Guests who pet Thumper or pick him up say,
a. "Oops! I thought that was your cat, but it's a furry basketball."
b. "Are cats supposed to weigh twenty-five pounds?"
c. "What a great lap cat! He's just the right size."

Thumper's physical condition could best be described as
a. A heavy layer of fat covering the ribs, with a chubby face and fatty deposits at the abdomen and the base of the tail. Some areas of skin are dry and scaly, because Thumper can't reach them to groom himself.
b. A rounded stomach and ribs that can be felt only by pushing through a layer of fat. Thumper is the poster model for the local Weight Watchers' group.
c. Muscular and well proportioned, with minimal abdominal fat and a

waist that is observable behind the ribs. Thumper is the mascot at the local gym.

If you answered with mostly *a* or *b* descriptions, your Thumper probably fits the profile of an overweight cat: a neutered male mixed-breed housecat between the ages of four and ten with an obsessive interest in food. If you answered *c* to all the questions, you probably have an average healthy adult cat weighing 8 to 10 pounds.

Feline physiology is much like that of humans. When cats get fat, health problems are not far behind. A fat cat is more likely to develop diabetes; the excess weight it carries stresses joints, ligaments and tendons; it is less able to tolerate heat; and it runs a higher risk of anesthetic and surgical complications.

Why do cats get fat? Forget myths about spaying and neutering causing obesity. The answer is simple: Fat cats eat too much, and they don't get enough exercise. The cat food sold today is specially formulated to appeal to cats, and many owners offer the food on a constant basis, assuming their cats will regulate their intake. The indoor cat's sedentary lifestyle is another factor. Although adult cats aren't as active as kittens, their owners feed them the same amount of food. The tendency toward obesity is also fueled by owner attitudes and misconceptions, such as the desire to please the cat or the belief that it is normal for a cat to put on weight as it ages. Whatever the cause, the fact remains that obesity and ill health go paw in paw. A fat cat is no laughing matter.

Putting Thumper on a Diet

Before you decide to cut Thumper's calories, take him to the veterinarian for a checkup. It's important to make sure that there isn't a medical reason for his weight gain. Ask your veterinarian for her advice on how much weight Thumper should lose and how quickly he should shed the pounds. Rapid weight loss is dangerous; remember that your goal is to safely return Thumper to a healthy size.

Most of us know from experience that a diet is easy to start and difficult to continue. The same is true for cats. They are creatures of habit and dislike change. To make the experience easier on both of you, try the following tips.

- **Make the change gradually.** If you are switching to a weight-reduction food, don't do it all at once. Mix in small amounts of the new food with the old, adding a little more of the new food each day. By the tenth day, Thumper should be eating only the diet food.

- **Disguise the change.** There are two ways to reduce your cat's weight: Feed less food or feed a food that is lower in calories. If you equate food with love, it may be easier for you to feed Thumper the same amount of a weight-reduction food than to give him less of his regular food. The other option is to feed a lesser amount of the same food. If you use a measuring cup to scoop out dry food, simply replace it with one of a smaller size.

- **Don't make too drastic a change.** If Thumper is used to getting canned food, don't abruptly switch him to dry food.

- **Prevent overeating.** Keep an eye on Thumper to make sure he doesn't steal food from other pets. It may be easiest to feed him in a separate area. Be sure the whole family understands that Thumper is on a diet and that they are not to feed him treats or table scraps. Explain the health risks involved with being overweight, especially if you have children who worry that Thumper isn't getting enough to eat.

- **Give Thumper an incentive to eat.** If he turns up his nose at the new food, warm it in the microwave or enhance the flavor with a small amount of water, low-fat chicken broth or the juice from waterpacked salmon or tuna (don't use milk).

- **Feed several small meals daily.** The mere act of eating burns calories, so a cat that eats more frequently burns a greater number of calories. The extra meals will help ease Thumper's hunger pangs and make him think he's getting more food than he actually

is. This also helps prevent begging, a behavior that should go unrewarded. Don't set down the food bowl until the begging behavior stops.

- **Stick to a schedule.** Feed set amounts at set times. To prevent obesity in the first place, avoid free-feeding with any cat that is obsessed with food.

- **Don't withhold treats.** Nutrition experts advise people who are dieting not to deprive themselves of favorite foods but instead to eat them in moderation. Treat Thumper the same way. Offer healthy, low-calorie treats such as raw vegetables—broccoli, carrots or green beans—or fruit, such as cantaloupe, grapes or apples. Whenever your cat receives treats, reduce its regular food by the appropriate amount.

- **Schedule regular weigh-ins.** Chart Thumper's progress weekly. The information will help you determine if you are feeding the appropriate amount.

Your cat should not lose more than two tenths of a pound per week. To weigh your cat, first stand on the scales while you are holding the cat, then without it. The difference is how much your cat weighs. A monthly weigh-in by your veterinarian is a good idea, too. He can advise you on adjusting the amount of food, if necessary.

- **Lose the guilt.** It's important to distinguish your emotions from Thumper's. Thumper may react negatively when you serve him diet food instead of scrambled eggs with smoked salmon, but it is because the food is different, not because he is angry with you.

Choosing a Diet Food

In the 1980s, a number of pet food manufacturers developed weight-loss diets for cats. Generally, these foods contain less fat and more carbohydrates or fiber.

This is necessary for weight reduction because fat contains more than twice as many calories as carbohydrates or protein. Less fat means fewer calories, even if the amount of food is the same.

Unfortunately, cat food labels are not required to list the total amount of fat or calories the food contains, but you can obtain this information by calling the manufacturer at the toll-free number listed on the bag or can. Ideally, a weight-reduction food will contain 8 to 11 percent fat on a dry-matter basis. Don't rely on the terms "light" or "lite." A study of fifteen commercially available brands at Cornell University's Feline Health Center showed that some "light" foods contain more fat and calories than regular foods. Compare the fat and calorie levels of several products to determine which is best for your cat's needs. The recommended feeding regimen for cats is 32 calories per pound of body weight daily. If Thumper's ideal weight is 10 pounds, he should receive no more than 320 calories per day.

Whether you should go with a diet high in carbohydrates or high in fiber is a matter of choice. Complex carbohydrates such as corn and rice are easy to digest. Fiber provides bulk, which is believed to help cats feel full, even though they have taken in fewer calories. However, cat food manufacturers and veterinary nutritionists are split on whether high amounts of fiber effectively help cats lose weight. One concern is that too much fiber can cause diarrhea or excessive stool production. Remember that cats are individuals. You may have to try several foods before you find one that works for your cat.

Yes, Cats Need Exercise

Controlling your cat's food intake and exercise level can help keep it in tip-top condition. A healthy cat that is kept indoors can live to be fifteen years or older. But don't let your kitty become a couch potato. Even an indoor cat needs regular exercise. By providing a variety of toys and scheduling daily playtime, you can ensure that your cat gets the activity it needs.

Cats like toys that are interactive—things they can chase, pounce on, bat around. Toys that make noise are good, too, especially if the noise is high-pitched, mimicking the sound a cat's prey might make. Special favorites include fishing pole–type toys, catnip-stuffed mice and Ping-Pong balls. Fishing pole toys are especially good for keeping your cat in shape. You will be amazed by the flips, twists and leaps your cat is capable of. If your cat likes to retrieve, toss a Ping-Pong ball or a piece of wadded-up paper. The erratic path of the Ping-Pong ball and the sound it makes on a bare floor will fascinate your cat. To prevent boredom, rotate toys weekly.

Provide a climbing area. A cat post should be a minimum of 36 inches high to permit your cat to stretch out to its full length. One that goes all the way to the ceiling is even better. To protect your carpet and furniture, consider buying a post covered in sisal. Cats love the texture and usually prefer it to other materials.

For safe outdoor exercise, teach your cat to wear a leash and harness so it can accompany you on a daily walk. Siamese cats and other Oriental breeds are especially amenable to leash-training. An enclosed cat run is another way to safely let your cat stretch its legs outdoors. This allows your cat to enjoy fresh air and a larger play area, but protects it from roaming cats that may be diseased, coyotes and other predators (who, after all, are just trying to get their daily meal), and people with less than friendly intentions.

While it plays, observe your cat closely. There is no better time to appraise its physical condition. Is Thumper energetic and willing to play for long periods, or does he tire quickly or begin to breathe heavily after only a few minutes? Do his eyes easily follow the course of the line on the fishing pole? Changes in your cat's ability or desire to play should be discussed with your veterinarian. They may indicate a health problem.

Remember that a flexible body and a flexible mind are intertwined. Stimulating Thumper's body with exercise can increase blood flow to the organs, prevent obesity, and keep him lithe and lively. Stimulating his brain with toys and games can increase his life expectancy. By controlling Thumper's diet and investing only five minutes a day of playtime, you can add years to your cat's life.

Keeping Your
Cat Healthy

CHAPTER 10

Many of the diseases seen in cats are linked to food or eating habits. Although food itself is not always the culprit, the cat's eating habits can provide clues to a condition, or they can cause it, as in the case of diarrhea.

Anorexia

A cat's loss of appetite and refusal to eat is cause for concern and should be immediately brought to the attention of your veterinarian. Cats are sensitive, and an unwillingness to eat may be a sign of illness or stress. Watch your cat and record any changes in eating habits; be prepared to tell your veterinarian about these changes. Then consider your surroundings and any recent changes that may have affected your cat. Blood and other tests may be required to find the problem's source. An appetite stimulant or feeding tube may be required to treat this problem.

Constipation

You know the signs. Your cat crouches in its litter box, straining to produce something. Finally, a few small, dry, hard stools appear. Sometimes, no matter how hard the cat tries or how many times it returns to the litter box, no stool is produced. Yes, your cat is constipated.

A low-fiber, high-meat-protein diet can result in chronic constipation. Hairballs are another cause, especially when the cat has long hair. Total fecal impaction occurs when the cat eats an undigestible substance such as paper or cloth.

Take your cat to the veterinarian as soon as you suspect constipation. She may recommend a high-fiber food, the addition of a bulk-forming laxative such as wheat bran or Metamucil to the cat's food, or a lubricant such as Laxatone or other medications. Fecal impaction may require an enema, which should be administered only by a veterinarian.

Dental Disease

Cavities aren't common in cats, but periodontal disease is. It occurs most frequently in cats that eat primarily a canned or semi-moist diet. The residue from food forms a soft film of bacteria-filled mucus on the teeth called plaque. Plaque hardens into tartar, or calculus. Tartar buildup causes bad breath, loose teeth and even serious organ infections. To help scrape tartar off teeth, be sure your cat has a supply of abrasive treats such as hard biscuits, or access to dry food. Brushing your cat's teeth several times a week is the best way to prevent dental disease.

Diabetes

Is your cat drinking a lot of water, constantly running to the litter box, and eating ravenously yet losing weight? It may have diabetes. Many people are surprised to learn that cats can develop diabetes, but it is a common condition, especially in overweight cats. Diabetes occurs when the pancreas is unable to produce enough insulin, a hormone that cells need to convert sugar to energy.

If you notice these signs in your cat,

take it to the veterinarian immediately. A simple blood and urine test can diagnose the condition.

Diarrhea

From poisons to parasites, disease to diet, loose or liquid stools can have a number of causes. Most commonly, however, the culprit is dietary. A cat can get diarrhea from eating inappropriate table scraps, getting into garbage, eating nonfood items such as feathers, or eating too much of any food, even its regular diet. A rapid or unexpected change in diet can also bring on diarrhea. Fortunately, cats are pretty picky about what they eat, so it's unusual for them to ingest toxic substances that can cause diarrhea.

When a cat develops diarrhea, withhold its food (but not water) for one day. Then feed it a bland meal of equal amounts of boiled chicken and rice. If the runny stools continue, take your cat to the veterinarian right away. Severe diarrhea can cause dehydration, and it is a common sign of intestinal disease, so it should not be ignored.

Feline Lower Urinary Tract Disease

Cats with feline lower urinary tract disease (FLUTD) squat and strain to urinate, but try as they might, they produce little or no urine. Or they may urinate frequently, often breaking litter box training because they can't make it there in time; pass bloody urine; cry from pain as they urinate; or lick their penis or vulva frequently. If this continues untreated, the body is unable to eliminate toxic wastes, the cat loses its appetite, kidney damage occurs, and eventually the cat dies. Relieving the obstruction as quickly as possible is critical.

Blockage occurs because the urethra is plugged with crystalline formations, or mucus, and red and white blood cells. Factors that affect crystal formation include high levels of magnesium in the urine, or urine with a high (or alkaline) pH. Both the magnesium level and the can be influenced by diet. Other factors may include obesity, low water intake and poor litter box maintenance, which results in the cat urinating less often than it should.

To treat FLUTD, your veterinarian will probably recommend a change in diet, to a food that is low in magnesium. Many companies produce foods that help prevent the recurrence of FLUTD. High-magnesium foods that should be avoided include fish, shellfish, cheese, table scraps, and vitamin or mineral supplements. If the change in diet is unsuccessful, surgery may be the only recourse.

Food Allergy

Just like people, cats can get allergies. Some cats are sensitive to certain foods. Most commonly, they react to beef, chicken, corn, eggs, fish, milk, pork, soy and wheat. Signs of food allergy include an itchy rash on the head, neck and back; swollen eyelids; or hair loss and oozing sores caused by frequent scratching. Less common signs are vomiting shortly after eating, or watery diarrhea.

To diagnose a food allergy, your veterinarian may recommend what is called an elimination diet. This means the cat must eat only a food that contains ingredients to which it has never been exposed. After about eight weeks, the veterinarian will reintroduce foods, one at a time. If symptoms reappear, you will know your cat is allergic to that particular food, and you should eliminate it from his diet.

Hepatic Lipidosis

You might think that it's a good thing when a fat cat refuses to eat, but the result can be hepatic lipidosis, a life-threatening condition that is unique to cats. Stress combined with obesity are factors in the development of hepatic lipidosis, which is a common cause of liver failure. As little as two or three days without food can cause fat to accumulate in liver cells, enlarging and damaging the liver. If your cat isn't eating, report the situation to your veterinarian immediately. Treatment requires fluid replacement, appetite stimulants and force feeding if necessary.

Hyperthyroidism

Your old cat eats well, he's bright and alert, and he's unusually active. He must be in good health, right? Not necessarily. If you look a little deeper, you may notice that the activity consists of restless and irritable pacing. Despite his good appetite, he is losing weight. One of the most common hormonal disorders of older cats, hyperthyroidism kicks in when the thyroid gland begins to produce too much thyroid hormone (thyroxin). This is a problem in old cats, because the extra thyroxin increases the heart's workload and the metabolic rate of the entire body.

Hyperthyroidism is diagnosed with blood testing, and there are three forms of treatment: antithyroid medication, surgical removal of the thyroid gland, or radioactive iodine treatment, which is the most successful of the three therapies.

Megacolon

Some cats lose the ability to achieve contractions in the colon. The lack of contractions renders the cat unable to empty its bowel. When this happens, the cat's colon becomes enlarged as it fills with feces. Some cats are able to cope with this condition with the help of medicine, while other cats require surgery to remove the enlarged colon.

Megaesophagus

When is a cat like a pelican? When it has megaesophagus. This condition is also called dilated esophagus, and that term is very descriptive. When megaesophagus develops, food builds up in the esophagus instead of going on to the stomach. As more food accumulates there, the esophagus becomes distended, stretching like a balloon. Not surprisingly, cats with megaesophagus regurgitate the undigested food, lose weight and may develop aspiration pneumonia from inhaling food into their breathing tubes.

There are many causes for megaesophagus. A kitten that develops it usually has a defective esophagus or defective heart development leading to obstruction of the esophagus. Congenital megaesophagus may be hereditary. Adult cats can get megaesophagus when foreign bodies lodge or tumors form in the esophagus, or it can be caused by diseases of the nervous system or the immune system, or by heavy metal poisoning.

Ways to treat megaesophagus include raising the height of the cat's dishes so that gravity helps the food go down, and feeding food in a semiliquid form. Some types of megaesophagus can be treated with surgery or medication.

Salmonella Poisoning

A common misconception is that cats prefer raw food, and that it is healthy for them. However, a USDA publication advises consumers to assume that most raw foods of animal origin are contaminated with salmonella bacteria. These bacteria can cause food poisoning and gastrointestinal inflammation, so you should never feed your cat raw eggs, meat or poultry, no matter how "natural" a diet it may seem.

Salmonella poisoning is potentially zoonotic, meaning it can be transmitted not only to other cats but also to humans. Wash your hands frequently if you are dealing with a cat with salmonella poisoning, and clean the cat's food and water dishes after each use.

Toxoplasmosis

Cats that hunt for themselves may come home with more than a dead bird or mouse. They can also pick up the protozoan *Toxoplasma gondii* when they eat an infected animal. Raw or undercooked meat, such as beef, mutton, pork or veal, can also harbor this parasitic microorganism. Cats with toxoplasmosis usually show no signs of disease. The trouble

with toxoplasmosis is that, like salmonella poisoning, it can be transmitted from cats to humans. Pregnant women are especially at risk, and may want to consult their doctors about potential problems.

The best way to prevent toxoplasmosis is to keep your cat indoors, so it can't roam and hunt. Avoid feeding raw meat. The feces of an infected cat are a source of infection to people, so pregnant women should avoid scooping the litter box (one of the benefits of pregnancy). There is no need, however, to get rid of the cat, especially if it stays safely indoors. Your veterinarian can test the cat for exposure to toxoplasma. A positive test result indicates active immunity, meaning that the cat is unlikely to transmit the disease to humans.

Vitamin E Deficiency

Cats have a reputation for being fish lovers, but fish doesn't always agree with them. When cats eat a diet consisting primarily of fish, especially tuna, a serious deficiency of vitamin E can be the result. A cat suffering from vitamin E deficiency acts depressed, loses its appetite and may have intense abdominal pain. Fortunately, this condition is rare, and treatment is easy: vitamin E supplements and a switch to a more balanced diet.

Vomiting/Upset Stomach

One of the most common reasons a cat vomits is hairballs. Brushing your cat several times a week may reduce excess hair that your cat ingests when it performs its grooming ritual. Cats under stress may also vomit frequently. A recent move, a new baby or pet, schedule changes, guests, or even owner stress all may cause a sensitive cat to vomit. Other cats may gorge their food, eating too quickly and then vomiting. To combat this problem, a cat owner might want to feed small amounts of food, so that the cat doesn't eat too much too fast. Persistent vomiting can be a sign of many illnesses.